learning. exploring. discovering. learning. exploring. discovering. learning. exploring. discovering. learning. exploring. discovering. learning.

Italy

Children's travel activity and keepsake book

tinytourists

explore. discover. learn.

Ciao !

Hello! My name's Topher*
and I love adventures!

I'll be keeping you company on your journey through
this book. Look out for me, I'll be popping
up every now and again.

Count how many times
you can spot me...

*Topher is named after St. Chris**topher**, the patron saint for travellers who is known for keeping all those who travel safe from harm.

tinytourists is all about inspiring family travel and making the most of adventures; keeping travel meaningful and memorable, educational and fun. Visit us on Facebook to find out more and to join the tinytourists' community.

Written and Designed by Louise Amodio
Illustrated by Louise Amodio and Catherine Mantle
Cover Illustrations by Giacomo (age 8), Emma (age 5), Luca (age 7), Isabella (age 5).

Published by Beans and Joy Publishing Ltd as a product from Tiny Tourists Ltd, Great Britain.
www.beansandjoy.com

ISBN: 978-0-9954949-5-4

This book belongs to:

Design your own suitcase

Your adventure starts here

How to use this book

Welcome to your fun-packed travel activity book!

Look out for these symbols to tell you what type of activity you'll be doing so you can start to work independently:

 for writing and mark-making

 for drawing and colouring and being creative

Time to get started!

For the grown-ups to read:

Section 1: My Travel Log

Use this section to start thinking about your trip to Italy; when you're going, where you're going, who you're going with, what the weather be like, and what you'll pack in your suitcase. This will help form part of a lovely keepsake as well as practice your planning and organisational skills!

Section 2: Explorer Skills

This section is full of games and activities for a bit of Italy-themed fun. All are designed to support the National Curriculum and are grouped into **Maths (p12-25), Literacy (p26-36), and The World Around Us (p37-42)**. See index for more details.

Also included are some italian words you might like to try out during your trip. We give you the true spelling, the phoentic spelling, and the english translation to make things straightforward.

phrase: ciao
say: (chow)
meaning: hello

phrase: grazie
say: (grazi-eh)
meaning: thank you

phrase: por favor
say: (poor fav-or)
meaning: please

Section 3: Memory Bank

This is where you can record all the memories from your trip. The perfect finishing touch to a lovely book of holiday memories; what you did, what you ate, what you saw, what you collected, and fun lists for recording the best bits and the worst bits.

Happy Travels!

My Travel Log

Me:

Stick or draw your picture here →

My Destination:

Arrival:

Date: _____

Passport Stamp:

Departure:

Date: _____

Where am I going?

This is a map of Italy.
Find out where you are going on holiday, any journeys you may
be taking, and add them to the map:

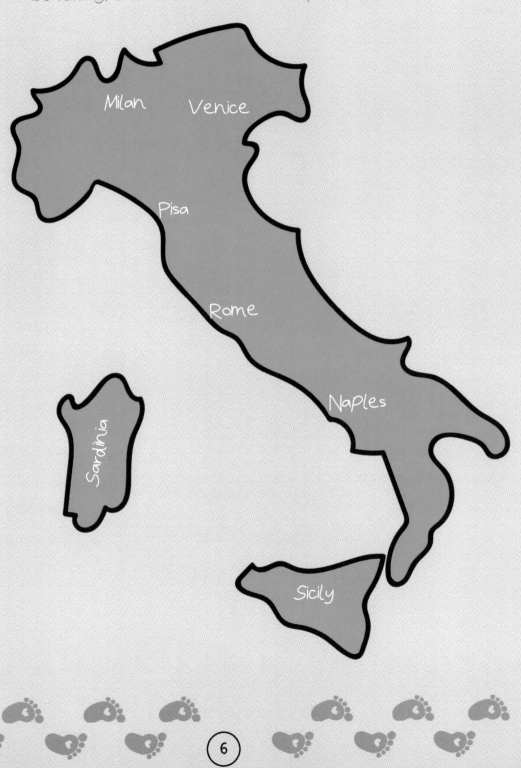

Milan

Venice

Pisa

Rome

Naples

Sardinia

Sicily

How will I get there?

Find the transport you're using to get to Italy and colour it in:

What am I taking with me?

Draw the important things you've got packed in your suitcase:

La mia borsa
(la mia borsa)
My bag

Who am I going with?

Draw a picture of who you're going on holiday with in the frame below:

Example

Holiday Portrait

| La mia mama *(eel mia mamo)* My mummy | Il mio papa *(eel mio papa)* My daddy | Il mio fratello *(il mio fratelo)* My brother | La mia sorella *(la mia sorela)* My sister |

What will the weather be like?

Draw a circle around the weather you think you'll have:

Piove
(pee-of-ay)
It's raining

C'e il sole
(che il solay)
It's sunny

Sta nevicando
(sta nevi cando)
It's snowing

Explorer Skills

Get equipped to be a tiny tourist!

Problem-solving
(Maths)

Code-breaking
(Literacy)

Spy Skills
(The World
Around Us)

Il Tricolore

This is the Italian flag, with 3 colours, green, white and red.
Complete the flag below by adding green and red stripes.

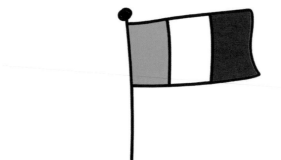

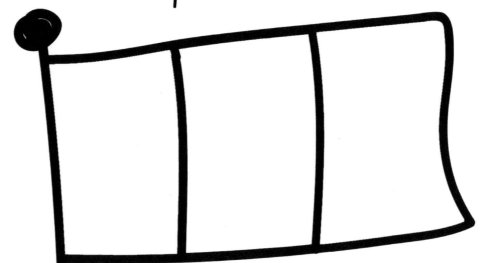

verde
(vair-de)
green

bianco
(bee-anco)
white

rosso
(ross-o)
red

Red Ferrari

Ferraris are one of Italy's most famous make of car.
They are known for going fast and looking sporty.

Circle all the **red** Ferrari cars.
How many are there?

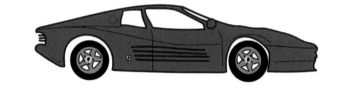

3

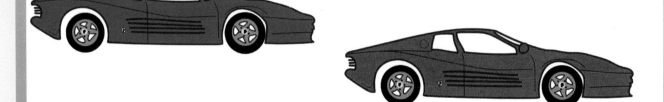

Green Lamborghini

Lamorghinis are another make of Italian sports car.

Circle all the **green** Lamborghini Cars.
How many are there?

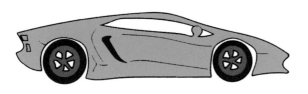

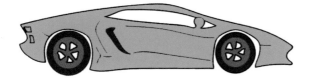

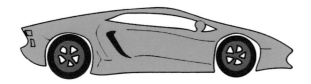

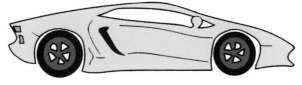

Design your own Ferrari

You may spot a Ferrai during your time in Italy.
Would you like to own your own Ferrari one day?
Design the Ferrais below in your own choice of colours:

la macchina
(la ma-kin-a)
car

Insalate Caprese 1-5

Italy's most famous salad, Caprese Salad, is made up of three ingredients the colours of the Italian flag: red tomatoes, green basil and white mozzarella. You might see it in restaurants and cafes while you are in Italy.

Count the ingredients below and circle the right number on the number line:

1 2 3 4 5

il pomodoro
(eel pom-or-doro)
tomato

1 2 3 4 5

il basilico
(eel basilico)
basil

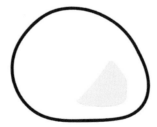

1 2 3 4 5

la mozzarella
(la mozzarella)
mozzarella

Insalate Caprese 1-10

Count the ingredients and **circle the right number** below.
Which one do you think is your favourite?
Do you think this food is healthy or not healthy?

1 2 3 4 5 6 7 8 9 10

1 2 3 4 5 6 7 8 9 10

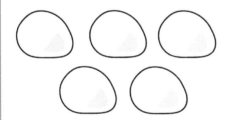

1 2 3 4 5 6 7 8 9 10

uno	due	tres	quattro	cinqe	sei	siete	otto	nove	dieci
uno	*do-ay*	*tre*	*qua-tro*	*chinkweh*	*say*	*seteh*	*otto*	*novay*	*dee-etchi*
1	2	3	4	5	6	7	8	9	10

E Buono 1-5

You will probably get to try many delicious Italian foods on your travels. If you like what you taste you can say "E Buono" (eh bwono) which means "it's tasty/it's good".

Count the parmesan cheese, olives, mushrooms and pepperoni below and **circle the right number** on the number line:

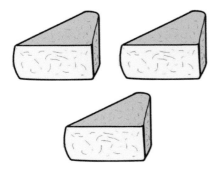

1 2 3 4 5

formaggio
(for-ma-jee-o)
cheese

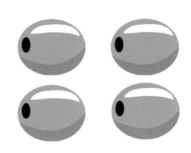

1 2 3 4 5

olive
(ol-ee-vay)
olives

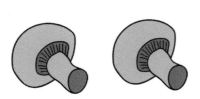

1 2 3 4 5

funghi
(foon-gi)
mushrooms

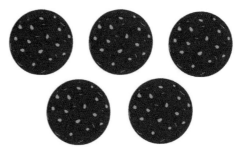

1 2 3 4 5

peperoni
(peperoni)
pepperoni

E Buono 1-10

Count these foods and **circle the right number** below.

Which is your favourite?

1 2 3 4 5 6 7 8 9 10

1 2 3 4 5 6 7 8 9 10

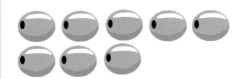

1 2 3 4 5 6 7 8 9 10

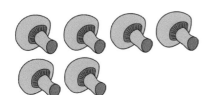

1 2 3 4 5 6 7 8 9 10

uno	due	tres	quattro	cinqe	sei	siete	otto	nove	dieci
uno	*do-ay*	*tre*	*qua-tro*	*chinkweh*	*say*	*seteh*	*otto*	*novay*	*dee-etchi*
1	2	3	4	5	6	7	8	9	10

Pizza!

Pizza is one of Italy's most famous foods. It has a bread base and is normally topped with a tomato sauce, cheese and then other toppings.

What are your favourite pizza toppings?
Add your favourite toppings to the pizza base below:

Pizzeria matching Pairs

A pizza restaurant is called a Pizzeria. Help the pizzeria owner make sure he has enough ingredients for a pizza he is making. He needs two of each ingredient.

Draw a line between each matching pair below.

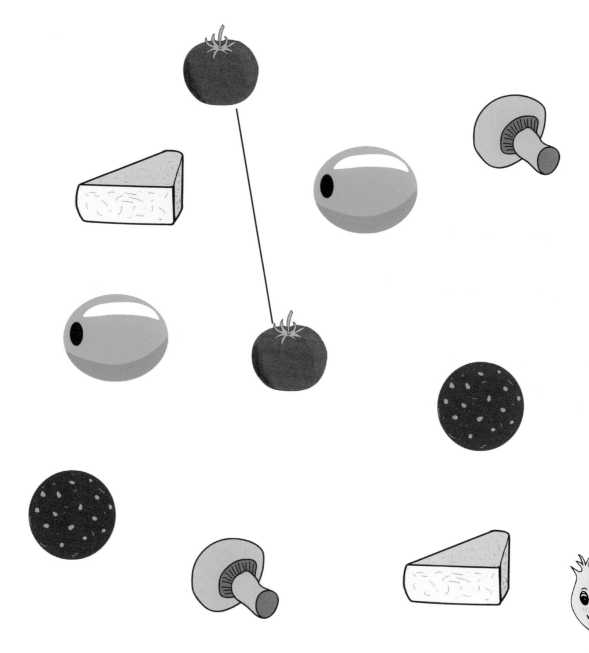

Lago di Garda

Lake Garda is the biggest lake in Italy.
See if you can **find the smallest boat** on this lake.

Smallest

Can you **circle** the smallest boat on each of these rows?

piccola
(pick-o-la)
small

barca
(barka)
boat

Skiing in Italy

Italy has many mountains which people love to ski down.

Find the biggest skier on this ski slope:

24

Biggest

Can you **circle** the biggest skier on each of these rows?

grande
(grond-ey)
big

The Colosseum

This building is a really old oval-shaped theatre, used by the Emperors of Rome to host battles between trained fighters called gladiators. Elephants, lions, tigers, rhinos, giraffes and bears were also brought to Rome to fight in these battles.

Much of the Colosseum has now fallen down, but you can still visit. You can even go into the tunnels underneath it and see the 36 trapdoors in the ground that were used to sneak new fighters into the ring.

Use your colouring pencils to **add some colour** to this picture. You might also want to draw some of the animals that used to work here:

The Leaning Tower of Pisa

In a town called Pisa there is a tower that looks like it's falling over. It started to lean when they were building it but they made it safe and now it is one of the most famous buildings in Italy. But it still leans!

Use your colouring pencils to **add some colour** to this picture:

Gondolas in Venice

There is a city in Italy called Venice that is mostly under water. To get from one place to another you often have to go by boat rather than by car, and go under lots of bridges. The boats are called Gondolas.

In the maze below, **draw a line** from the gondola all the way to the bridge:

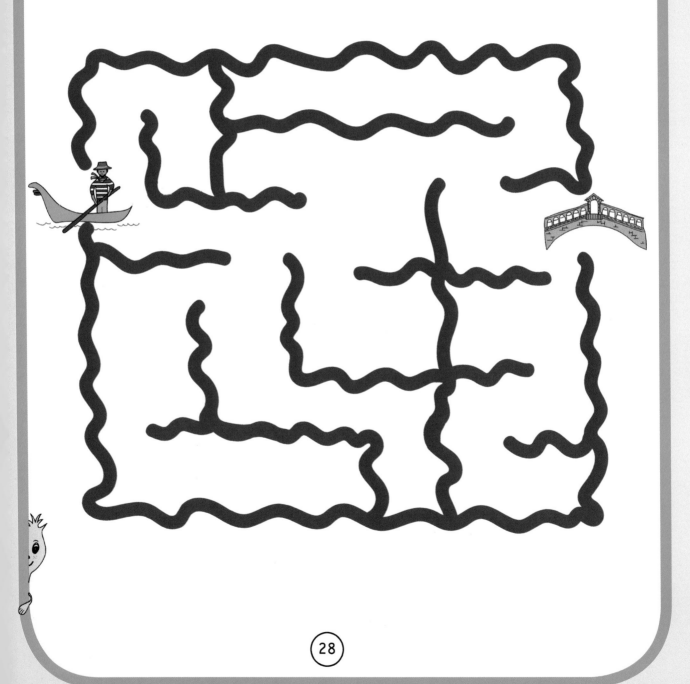

Gondola Tangle

Can you **trace along the dotted lines** to find out which gondola is headed for the bridge?

Shopping!

Italy is well-known for its fashion houses that make beautiful clothes, shoes and handbags. Many are based in a city called Milan in the north of Italy. This is a great place to go shopping!

Can you **trace your way** through the maze to help this lady find a new handbag to buy?

Shoes and Handbags

Can you match these shoes to the handbag of the same colour? **Draw a line** to join them together:

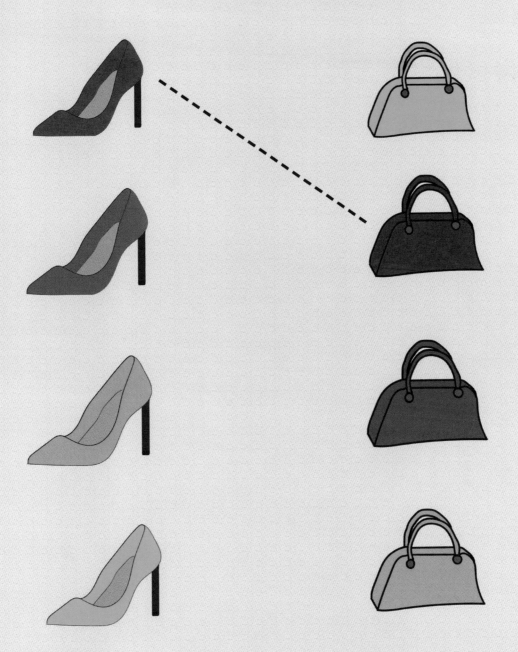

una scarpa
(oona skarp-a)
a shoe

una borsa a mano
(oona borsa a mano)
a handbag

Romeo and Juliet

There is a famous love story set in Italy, where a girl called Juliet falls in love with a boy called Romeo. Their families are arch-enemies which makes it difficult for them to see each other but they sneak out to meet up and fall in love for ever after.

What do you think Romeo is saying to Juliet in this picture?

Romeo and Juliet

Colour this picture matching the colours opposite, or in your own choice of colours:

Shape-search

Find the objects in this grid that look like circles and triangles. How many are there? Do you recognise any other shapes?

 _____    _____

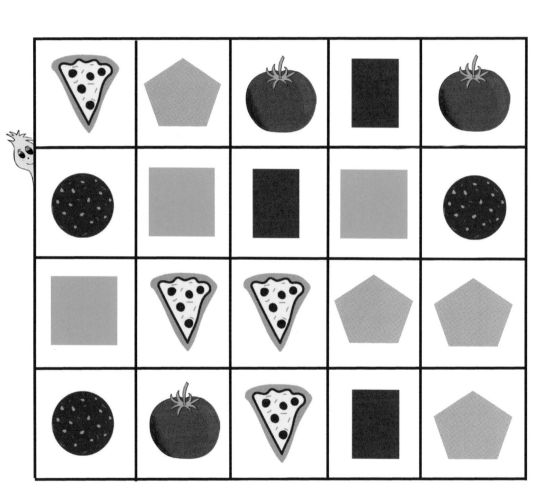

Letter-search Italia

Find as many of these 3 letters in the grid as you can:

i _ t _ a _

i	a	a	i	s
t	i	t	c	i
i	o	a	a	s
a	a	t	u	t

Italian beaches

All along Italy's coastline, and around its islands, such as Sardinia and Sicily, there are many beaches to enjoy.

Can you write your name in the sand below?

Gelato!

No visit to Italy is complete without a taste of a delicious ice-cream, called un gelato. Which is your favourite flavour?

In each row of ice-creams below try to **spot the one that's different** and draw a circle around it:

un gelato
(un jel-a-to)
an ice-cream

Volcano spot the difference

Italy is home to 20 volcanoes! Only two are currently erupting. They are called Mount Etna and Mount Stromboli and both can be found on islands in the south of Italy.

Volcano spot the difference

Can you spot the 5 differences between these two volcanoes?

A Place to Stay

Where are you staying on your holiday in Italy? Is it a hotel? A house? A tent? A boat? A campervan? An apartment?

Can you **draw a picture** of it here?

Home Sweet Home

Can you **draw a picture** of where you live back at home?

What is different about this and your holiday home?

What do you know about Italy?

Can you **circle** some of the things you might see in Italy?
Which things do you think you might NOT see?

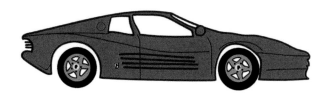

Memory Bank

Use this section to record and remember all the
things you've done, seen and tasted on your trip!

You may need a grown up to
help with some of the writing...

What have you eaten?

Draw some food you have eaten on holiday on the plate below.
What was your favourite?

What adventures have you had?

Ask someone to help you **write a postcard** about your adventures, and design a nice stamp:

Cartolina Postale

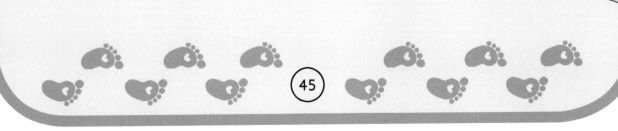

Momento Collage

Stick bits and pieces on these pages that you've collected during your trip; favourite tickets, receipts, leaflets, drawings, flowers...

Daily Diary

Note down some of the different things you have done each day:

Monday

Tuesday

Wednesday

Thursday

Friday

Saturday

Sunday

Memory Gallery

Draw pictures or doodles of any special memories:

Worst 5

What have been the **worst** five things about your trip?

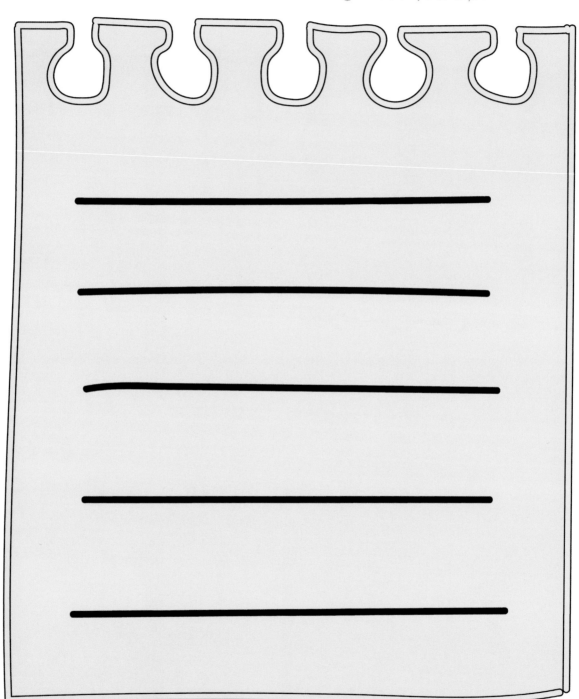

_____

_____

_____

_____

_____

Top 5

What have been the **best** five things about your trip?

Index

(what's in this book and where you can find it)

Arriverderci

(goodbye, until next time)

I hope you enjoyed your adventure and completing this book along the way.

How many times did you spot me?

_____

Where would you like to go next?

Spain

USA

Greece

France

Egypt

China

UK

Australia

South Africa

Thailand

Mexico

Finland

34034184R00031

Printed in Great Britain
by Amazon